THE SCOTSMAN

Collins

SCOTTISH

WORDS

Collins

HarperCollins Publishers
Westerhill Road
Bishopbriggs
Glasgow
G64 2QT

www.collinslanguage.com

First Edition 2009

This edition created exclusively
for The Scotsman

ISBN 978-0-00-785550-6

A–Z text © HarperCollins
Publishers 2009

Introduction © John Abernethy
2009

Illustrations © Alex Collier
2009

The moral rights of the author
have been asserted

The moral rights of the
illustrator have been asserted

A catalogue record for this
book is available from the
British Library.

Designed and typeset by
Thomas Callan

Printed in Great Britain by
Clays Ltd, St Ives plc

Editor
Mike Munro

Editorial Staff
Ian Brookes
Helen Hucker
Cormac McKeown

For the Publishers
Lucy Cooper
Elaine Higgleton

Introduction

Join us on a 'dander' from the 'barry' denizens of
Edinburgh and the 'gallus' folk of Glasgow, taking
a detour 'doon-bye' to the Borders and Dumfries
& Galloway and then, ensuring that you have first
remembered to take your 'piece' with you, 'gang'
north through the 'braes', 'lochs' and 'glens' of the
'couthy' Highlands, where you might spend an
evening or two on the 'randan' before reaching the
'rowie' loving 'quines' and 'loons' of the North East
and beyond to the 'simmer dim' of Orkney and
Shetland.

On the way you may occasionally become a little
'crabbit' and even slightly 'black-affrontit' and you
may be so 'scunnered' by the occasionally 'dreich'
Scottish weather that you feel like having a 'greet', but
by the end of the journey if previously you knew 'heehaw' about Scottish words, you might feel slightly
'wabbit' from your exertions, but hopefully you will
have been 'awfy' entertained, and 'jings, crivvens' be
more conversant in the wonderful and 'weel-kent'
language that is Scots.

Slainte mhath and lang may yer lum reek

John Abernethy
2009

Pronunciation guide

Where the pronunciation of a word is unusual or of interest, guidance has been provided for the reader. The system used is self-explanatory, as far as possible, but the pronunciation guide below may be used in case of doubt.

Single vowels indicate a short sound. Longer vowels are indicated using the following letter-combinations:

ah	as in ma
air	as in fair
ar	as in car
aw	as in saw
ay	as in say
i(-)e	as in mile
ee	as in see
eer	as in beer
er	as in her
oe	as in toe
oo	as in tooth
or	as in for
ow	as in how
oy	as in boy
uh	as in the

Single consonants have their normal value, with other sounds being indicated by the following letter-combinations:

CH	a guttural sound, as in loch
ch	as in chew
dh	a soft sound, as in they
sh	as in show
th	as in thing
wh	an aspirated sound, like 'hw'

Readers should note that the letter 'r' is sounded when it follows a vowel in words such as 'for', and so the words 'sore' and 'saw' are pronounced differently in Scots, whereas an English speaker would make them sound the same.

A–Z of Scottish Words

agley or **aglee** *adverb, adjective* squint, askew or wrong: *The best laid schemes o' mice an' men gang aft agley.* (BURNS)

airt *noun* a direction or point of the compass: *The centre attracts visitors from a' the airts.*

ashet *noun* a large plate or shallow dish for cooking or serving food: *I'd rather have an ashet pie than a Scotch pie.* [French **assiette** plate]

awfy or **awfu** *adjective, adverb* awful or very: *They've made an awfy mess; She's awfy clever, that lassie.*

baffies *plural noun* slippers: *She's no away doon the shops wi they auld baffies on!*

baggie or **baggie minnie** *noun* a minnow, especially a large one: *When I was wee we used tae bring hame baggies in a jeely-jaur.*

bahookie or **behouchie** (*pronounced* ba-**hoo**-kee) a jocular word for a person's backside: *Is this carry-on no a pain in the bahookie?*

bairn *noun* **1** a baby or young child. This is used in most parts of the country, except primarily West Central Scotland, where **wean** tends to be used instead: *The wife's expecting a bairn; The bairns came home from the school.* **2** a nickname for a person from Falkirk [sense 2 springs from Falkirk's town motto: 'Better meddle wi the deil than the bairns o' Falkirk']

ballop (*pronounced* **bal**-op) *noun spoken in Galloway* the fly on a pair of trousers: *I suppose we'd better tell him his ballop's open.*

barkit (*pronounced* **bark**-it) *adjective spoken in Northeast* very dirty, especially encrusted with dried-on dirt: *Dinna put yer barkit boots on that chair!*

barrie or **barry** *adjective spoken in Edinburgh & Southeast* good or attractive: *Your hair looks really barrie like that.* [Romany]

bashit (*pronounced* **bash**-it) *adjective* mashed: *bashit neeps*

bauchle (*pronounced* **bawCH**-l) or **bachle** (*pronounced* **baCH**-l) *noun* literally a shabby or worn-out shoe, but mostly used to mean an ungainly or shabby-looking person, especially a small one: *He's a right wee bauchle.*

beastie *noun* a small animal, particularly an insect, spider, or similar creepy-crawly: *What's that beastie on the curtain?*

ben *noun* a mountain, often part of the mountain's name, such as Ben Nevis or Ben Lomond: *You could see all the nearby bens from the top of the hill.* | *preposition, adverb* in, within, or into the inner or main part of a house: *Come ben the hoose; She was ben the kitchen making tea.* [Gaelic]

bidie-in (*pronounced* bide-ee-**in**) *noun* somebody who lives with another person as their husband or wife although they are not married: *Katia Labeque, McLaughlin's bidie-in and sometime musical partner*

> This is a nicely informal way of describing such a relationship; much couthier than 'live-in lover' or 'fellow householder'.

bing *noun* a large hill-like mound of waste from a mine or quarry: *Large oil-shale bings disfigured the countryside.*

birk *noun* a birch tree: *the birks o' Aberfeldy*

birl *verb* to spin or revolve: *Ma heid's birlin wi aw this noise.*

black-affrontit (*pronounced* blak-a-**frunt**-it) or **black-affronted** *adjective* very embarrassed or offended: *He was* *black-affrontit when she told him his ballop was open.*

blaeberry (*pronounced* **blay**-ber-i) *noun* an edible purplish-black berry, also known as a bilberry or whortleberry: *They're away picking blaeberries.*

blaes (*pronounced* **blayz**) *noun* crushed hardened clay or shale, reddish or bluish-grey in colour, which is used to form the top layer of a sports ground: *a blaes pitch*

> Blaes is rather less fun to play on than grass – and definitely not for those unwilling to suffer a skint knee!

blaud (*pronounced* **blahd**) *verb spoken in Northeast* to spoil or damage: *a park o' blaudit neeps*

bleezin or **bleezin fou** *adjective spoken in Northeast* very drunk: *He wis fair bleezin.*

bodach (*pronounced* **boe**-daCH) *noun spoken in North & West* an old man: *Ask the bodach if he's wanting a dram.* [Gaelic]

boggin *adjective* very dirty: *Dinnae sit on the good chair in thae boggin troosers!*

boorach or **bourach** (*pronounced* **boo**-raCH) *noun* **1** *spoken in Northeast* a group of assorted people or things: *a boorach o' fowk* **2** *spoken in Highlands* a mess or a disorderly state or heap: *I've only been away a week and the house is a boorach.* [Gaelic]

bosie (*pronounced* **boe**-zi) *noun spoken in Northeast* **1** an embrace or cuddle: *Gie's a bosie.* **2** the bosom: *Stick that flooer in yer bosie.*

bowff or **bouff** (*pronounced* **bowf**) *verb* **1** to smell strongly and unpleasantly, like something rotten: *Eeugh! This beer's* *bowffin!* **2** to bark, or to speak or cough in a way that sounds like a dog barking: *Who's dug is yon that's aye bowffin?* | *noun* a strong unpleasant smell: *The bowff in that bedroom would sicken ye.*

brae (*pronounced* **bray**) *noun* a hill or hillside: *Set a stout hert tae a stey brae.*

braw *adjective* fine or excellent: *It's a braw day.* [a Scots form of **brave**]

breeks *plural noun* trousers or, occasionally, underpants: *Ma breeks're fallin doon!* [a Scots form of **breeches**]

breenge *verb* to go somewhere or do something in a hasty and forceful, usually clumsy, way: *He breenged his way through the crowd.* | *noun* a forceful but clumsy rush: *There'll be quite a breenge when these doors open.*

bubbly jock *noun* a male turkey [probably because of the noise it makes]

bumbaleerie (*pronounced* bum-buh-**lee**-ree) *noun* the backside: *Ach, sit on yer bumbaleerie!*

bumfle *noun* a wrinkle, crease, or fold in something: *Wait till I press the bumfles oot that shirt.* | *verb* to put wrinkles or creases in something: *My skirt had got all bumfled up at the back.* [from earlier Scots **bumph** meaning a lump or bump]

burn *noun* a stream or brook: *Is there fish in that burn?*

burny *adjective* extremely hot: *Use a cloth tae hold that dish; it's burny.*

buroo (*pronounced* buh-**roo** *or* **broo**) *or* **broo** *noun* the dole, or the office where people sign on for their dole money: *Has your buroo money come through yet?*; *He's been on the broo* *for years.* [from Employment *Bureau*, a former name for a Jobcentre]

but-and-ben (*pronounced* but-and-**ben**) *noun* an old-fashioned rural cottage consisting of two rooms, usually a kitchen and living room: *They're renting out the but-and-ben as a holiday cottage.*

buttery or **buttery rowie** *noun spoken in Aberdeen* a type of crumbly, butter-rich, bread roll: *Two cups of coffee and a couple of butteries, please.*

byke or **bike** (*pronounced* **bike**) *noun* a wasps' nest: *We had a wasps' byke in the attic last autumn.*

byordinar (*pronounced* bie-**or**-di-nar) *adjective, adverb* unusual or exceptionally: *a maist byordinar day; It's byordinar cauld for May.* [from *by* in the sense beyond, plus **ordinar** ordinary]

byre (*pronounced* **bire**) *noun* a shed or stable where cows are kept: *The kye are in the byre.*

cailleach (*pronounced* **kayl**-yaCH or **kal**-yaCH) *noun spoken in North & West* an old woman: *My memory of her is of a vague chain-smoking cailleach in eccentric garb and heavy henna.* [Gaelic]

caller (*pronounced* **kal**-er) *adjective* fresh, especially referring to fish, fruit, or vegetables: *caller herring*

camstairy (*pronounced* kam-**stair**-ee) or **camsteerie** (*pronounced* kam-**stee**-ree) *adjective* quarrelsome, stubborn, or unruly: *Let the camstairy auld deil dae whit he likes.*

cantrip *noun* **1** a spell or magic charm: *By some devilish cantrip slight, each in its cold hand held a light.* (BURNS) **2** a playful trick: *The bairns wouldnae be playin such cantrips if their faither was in the hoose.*

5

carnaptious (*pronounced* kar-**nap**-shuss) *adjective* grumpy, bad-tempered, or irritable: *She's a carnaptious auld biddy!* [from **knap** bite]

caul (*pronounced* **kawl**) *noun spoken in South* a weir or a dam: *A broken branch was stuck at the caul.*

causey (*pronounced* **kaw**-zi) *noun* **1** a cobbled street, road, or way: *That causey's awful slippy when it's rainin.* **2** a cobble or paving stone: *She's a lump on her heid the size o' a causey.*

ceud míle fáilte (*pronounced* **kee**-ut **mee**-luh **fah**-il-tya) *interjection* a hundred thousand welcomes: *He couldnae spell 'ceud míle fáilte' so he just wrote 'Hiya!'* [Gaelic]

> This greeting is often seen on place-name signs for towns, as if one, genuinely warm, welcome were not enough for anybody.

champit tatties *plural noun* mashed potatoes, one of the traditional accompaniments to haggis, along with bashit neeps, in a Burns Supper

chauve or **tyauve** (*pronounced* **chawv**) *spoken in Northeast verb* to struggle, strive, or work hard, often with little to show for one's exertions: *Still chauvin awa?* | *noun* a struggle: *It's a sair chauve for a half loaf.*

chookie or **chookie birdie** *noun* a bird: *Hear that wee chookie singin? That's a blackbird.*

chuckie or **chuckie stane** *noun* a stone or pebble of throwable size: *throwing chuckies in the water*

clabber or **glabber** *noun spoken in Southwest* mud, earth, or clay: *Ma trainers are still aw clabber fae T in the Park.* [Gaelic **clàbar** meaning mud or a puddle]

clachan (*pronounced* **klaCH**-an) *noun* a small village or hamlet: *He was born in a wee clachan in Argyll.* [Gaelic, meaning stone]

> This word was originally used only of Highland villages, but its use is now more widespread.

clack (*pronounced* **klak**) or **claick** (*pronounced* **klayk**) *spoken in Northeast noun* gossip or chat: *Never heed their daft clack.* | *verb* to gossip or chat: *How about some graftin, instead of clackin away like a pair o' sweetiewives?* [probably from one of its original meanings: the clattering sound of a mill in operation]

claes (*pronounced* **klayz**) *plural noun* clothes: *Hing on till Ah get some claes on.* The saying **back to auld claes and porridge** means a return to normality after a period of jollity, celebration, or indulgence: *After Hogmanay it's back to auld claes and porridge for us.*

clanjamfrie (*pronounced* klan-**jam**-free) or **clamjamfrie** (*pronounced* klam-**jam**-free) *noun* **1** a group of people, usually used to dismiss them as a rabble: *There's naebody wi' any sense in the hale clanjamfrie!* **2** a varied assortment of things; a mixed bag: *the clamjamfrie of tenements, courtyards and closes which forms Edinburgh's Old Town*

clapshot *noun* a dish of boiled potatoes and turnips which have been mashed together in roughly equal quantities: *Lunch is fillets of cod served with clapshot, roasted peppers, and chilli oil.*

cleg or **clegg** *noun* a horse-fly with a painful bite: *Once ye've been but wi' a cleg, ye're no feart o' midgies.* [Old Norse **klegge**]

clipshears or **clipshear** *noun* an earwig: *There was hundreds of clipshears and slaters under the flowerpot when she lifted it.* [from the resemblance of the pincers at the tip of the creature's abdomen to shears]

clishmaclaver (*pronounced* klish-ma-**clay**-ver) *noun* gossip or incessant chatter: *Ye should be ashamed o' yersel, repeatin clishmaclaver like yon!* [a combination of two Scots words, *clish* to repeat gossip, and *claver* to talk idly]

cloot *noun* a piece of cloth or a cloth used as a duster, etc: *Dicht roon the sink wi' a cloot.*

clootie dumpling (*pronounced* **kloo**-ti) *noun* a rich dark fruitcake served as a dessert, like a Christmas pudding. It is boiled or steamed in a **cloot** or cloth: *Ma grannie used tae pit a sixpenny bit in the clootie dumplin for some lucky soul tae find.*

cludgie (*pronounced* **kluj**-i) *noun spoken in Central* a toilet: *A wee boy's got locked in the cludgie.* [perhaps a mixture of *closet* and *ludge*, a Scots form of lodge]

clype *or* **clipe** *noun* a person who tells tales or informs on his or her friends, colleagues, or schoolmates: *Just you keep your mouth shut, ya wee clype!* | *verb* to tell tales or inform on: *We'd have been all right if she hadnae cliped on us tae the heidie.* [related to Old English *cleopian* to call or name]

coggle *verb* to wobble, rock, or be unsteady: *Tiger Woods' ball coggled for a minute on the lip of the eighteenth hole.*

coggly *adjective* shaky or unsteady: *Find another table; this yin's a wee bit coggly.*

collieshangie (*pronounced* kol-ee-**shang**-gee) *noun* a loud and disorderly commotion or quarrel: *What's all this collieshangie out in the street?* [the word used to mean a dogfight, so perhaps it comes from *collie* the breed of dog and *shangie* a chain or leash connecting two dogs]

connach (*pronounced* **kon**-naCH) *verb spoken in Northeast* **1** to spoil, in various different ways: *The crop was clean connached by the weather; He connacht the fairm wi his drinkin; The thunder connacht the milk; It wis his mither at aye connacht him.* **2** to tire out: *The wee lad wis fair connached wi the lang walk.* [perhaps from the old Gaelic *conach*, meaning a disease of cattle]

coorie *or* **courie** *verb* to nestle or snuggle: *He cooried in to his mother's side.* [from the Scots *coor* meaning cower]

corbie *noun* a crow: *twa corbies sittin on a wa'* [from Old French *corbin*]

coup *or* **cowp** (*pronounced* **kowp**) *noun* **1** a rubbish tip: *He's away tae the coup wi' his auld computer.* **2** a dirty or untidy place: *Tidy up that coup of a room of yours.* | *verb* to turn or fall over: *The wean couped her bowl onto the floor.* [from the Middle English *cowp* to strike]

couthy *or* **couthie** (*pronounced* **kooth**-i) *adjective* **1** plain, homely, or unsophisticated: *His poetry unaffectedly blended the couthy with the cosmopolitan.* **2** comfortable and snug: *They gave us a braw, couthy wee room on the ground floor.* **3** sociable and friendly: *They're such a couthy bunch that you'll soon make friends.* [from the Old English *cūth* known]

cowk *verb spoken in Northeast* to retch or vomit: *The sea got rough and ane or twa bairns were cowkin ower the side.*

crabbit (*pronounced* **krab**-it) *adjective* grumpy or bad-tempered: *He's aye crabbit first thing in the morning.* [a Scots form of *crabbed*]

crannie *noun spoken in Northeast* the little finger, or pinkie: *the size o' your crannie*

craw steps or **corbie steps** *plural noun* the small steps on the gable of a roof in traditional Scottish architecture: *We could make out the steeples and craw steps of the old town.*

creel *noun* a large basket used to carry bread or fish: *plenty herring to fill the creel* A **labster creel** is a wickerwork trap for catching lobsters and shellfish: *The fisherman told us that there was a labster creel on the seabed under each of the little buoys.*

creeshie *adjective* greasy or dirty: *Ah'm no eatin ony mair of thae creeshie burgers o' theirs.* [from **creesh** fat or tallow]

crivvens or **criffens** *interjection* an exclamation of surprise: *Crivvens, is that the time already?*

> This word is considered so inoffensive as to be quite suitable for ministers and aunties, even though some people think it was originally a form of **Christ defend us**.

crowdie (*pronounced* **krow**-di) *noun* a soft white cheese made by straining the whey from soured milk and beating up the remaining curd with salt: *The teashop served home-made scones with bramble jam amd crowdie.* [perhaps from **crud**, an earlier form of **curd**]

> It might be best to keep this rather unfortunate association with 'crud' at the back of your mind the next time you see crowdie on the menu.

cuddy or **cuddie** *noun* a donkey or a horse: *My legs are as stiff as an auld cuddy.* [possibly a nickname for **Cuthbert**, although that seems rather a high-falutin name for a donkey]

cundy *noun* the gutter at the side of the road or the cover of a drain: *The cundy was choked with dead leaves and rubbish.* [a Scottish pronunciation of the English *conduit*]

cushie-doo (*pronounced* koosh-ee-**doo**) or **cushat-doo** (*pronounced* koosh-at-**doo**) or **cushie** *noun* a wood pigeon: *Ah hear a cushie-doo cooin in yon tree, but Ah cannae spot it.* [from the English *cushat* plus *doo*, a Scots word for pigeon]

dachle (*pronounced* **daCH**-l) *verb spoken in Northeast* to dawdle or loiter: *Dinnae dachle on the road or it'll be dark afore ye get back.*

daffin *noun* playful or foolish behaviour: *He wis aye wan for daffin wi' the lassies.*

dander or **dauner** (*pronounced* **dawn**-er) *noun* a stroll: *I'm just away for a wee dander.* | *verb* to stroll: *You can dander across the Solway sands to Rough Island, but beware of being stranded by the incoming tide.*

darg *noun* a day's work or a task to be done: *He'll never ken the satisfaction o' finishin a good day's darg.* [from a contraction of **day-work**]

daud (*pronounced* **dawd**) or **dad** *noun* a lump or chunk of something: *Gie's a daud o' breid tae keep me goin.*

deave (*pronounced* **deev**) *verb* to deafen someone, or to bewilder or weary them with noise or talk: *Grandad was always deaving us with his war stories.*

deek *spoken in Edinburgh & Southeast verb* to look at or see something: *Deek this gadgie.* | *noun* a look at something: *Have a deek out the window.* [Romany]

deif (*pronounced* **deef**) *adjective* deaf: *I'm talking to you! Are ye deif or something?*

deil (*pronounced* **deel**) *noun* the devil: *They say the deil looks after his ain.*

dicht (*pronounced* **diCHt** *or* **dite**) *verb* to wipe something clean: *Dicht roon the sink.* | *noun* a wipe: *Gie your face a dicht.* [Old English *diht* to arrange]

diddy *noun* **1** a female breast or nipple: *a photie o' a lassie showin her diddies* **2** *spoken in Glasgow area* a foolish person: *D'ye know nothin, ya wee diddy?*

dirl *verb* to vibrate or shake: *The noise of the bagpipes made the very rafters dirl.*

disjaskit (*pronounced* dis-**jas**-kit) *adjective* miserable and unhappy, often being completely exhausted or worn out into the bargain: *He was in a maist disjaskit state.* [probably a variant of *dejected*]

doakie (*pronounced* **doe**-ki) *noun* a person's backside: *She gave the bairn a skelp on the doakie.*

docken (*pronounced* **dok**-en *or* **doe**-ken) *noun* **1** the dock plant or any of its leaves: *Rub that nettle-sting with a docken.* **2** a thing of no value or importance: *It's no worth a docken.*

doitit (*pronounced* **doyt**-it) *adjective* foolish or childish, often applied to older people suggesting that they are senile: *Ah've lost ma bus pass, doitit aul deil that Ah am!* [probably related to the English *dotage*]

donnert (*pronounced* **don**-nert) *adjective* stupid or stunned: *She was that donnert wi' the news she had tae sit doon.*

doo *noun* a dove, or even a lowly pigeon: *The weans were feedin the doos in George Square.*

dook *or* **douk** *verb* to duck, dip, or bathe: *a bonny white* *swan, dookin its heid intae the watter* | *noun* an act of ducking, dipping, or bathing: *Who's for a dook in the loch?*

doolie *noun* a foolish person: *Ye forgot tae stir the paint, ya doolie!*

doon-bye *adverb* down there, that is, in a place that has already been mentioned: *"Is it near Dumfries he stays?" "Aye, he lives doon-bye."*

dottled *adjective spoken in Northeast* confused, muddled or senile: *I may be old, but I'm no dottled yet.* [related to the English *dotage*]

doup (*pronounced* **dowp**) *noun* a person's buttocks: *Ye'll get a boot in yer doup if yer nae careful!* [Dutch *dop* a shell]

dowt *noun* a cigarette-end: *Some eejit flung a dowt intae the bushes and startit a fire.* [English dialect, meaning to put out a fire]

drappie *noun* a little drop, especially of spirits: *Then we had a drappie, just to make us happy.*

dree one's weird *phrase* to endure the fate that destiny has decreed for you: *Aye, it's hard luck on the lassie, but she'll just have to dree her weird like the rest of us.* [the main elements of this are essentially old English words: *dree* meaning to suffer, and *weird* meaning fate]

dreich (*pronounced* **dreeCH**) *adjective* **1** dreary or tedious: *It's one of the dreichest stretches of road in all Scotland.* **2** referring to weather, wet or dismal: *It's awful dreich this morning.*

> Anyone who spends a winter in Scotland will soon be able to identify weather that qualifies as dreich, and understand how fitting a term it is!

drookit or **droukit** (*pronounced* **drook**-it) *adjective* drenched or soaked: *The wee soul got caught in that rain and came in drookit.*

drooth or **drouth** *noun* a thirst: *You've got some drooth on ye the night!* [a Scots form of **drought**]

dwam or **dwaum** *noun* someone who is *in a dwam* is in a stupor or a daydream: *Sorry, I didn't catch what you said. I was away in a wee dwam.* [Germanic]

dwine *verb* to decline in health or vigour; to waste away: *At the rate she's dwining, the auld soul's not long for this world.* | *noun* a decline in health or vigour: *He went into a dwine and died the next day.*

eejit (*pronounced* **ee**-jit) *noun* an idiot: *There ought to be stronger measures taken to ban such eejits from being anywhere near guns.*

een *plural noun* eyes: *Ah havenae shut ma een a' nicht.* (One eye is an *ee*)

erse (*pronounced* **erss**) *noun* a person's backside: *Shift yer erse, wee man!*

ettle (*pronounced* **et**-l) *verb* to attempt to do something: *ettlin tae scrieve in Doric* [Old Norse]

fae (*pronounced* **fay**) or **frae** (*pronounced* **fray**) *preposition* from: *some guy fae Tollcross; Where'd he get that fae?*

> The east of Scotland punk band The Rezillos had a singer who called herself Fay Fife, thus economically allowing her name and place of origin to be identified simultaneously.

fankle *verb* to tangle something: *The fishing line had got all* *fankled up.* | *noun* a tangle or a state of confusion: *Don't get yourself in a fankle.*

fantoosh (*pronounced* fan-**toosh**) *adjective* ostentatious or pretentious: *Some of their outfits were awfy fantoosh.* [perhaps from the French *fantoche* a puppet]

farl *noun* a three-sided oatcake or piece of shortbread made by quartering a large round one: *The kind of scones I like best are soda farls.* [from the older *fardel* meaning a fourth part]

fash *verb* to trouble, bother, or annoy: *Dinna fash yersel.* [Old French]

faughie (*pronounced* **fawCH**-ee) *adjective spoken in North* pale and sickly-looking: *I thought she was lookin a wee bit faughie.*

faur (*pronounced* **for**) *adjective, adverb* far: *Ye're faur better gaun the Stirling road.*

feart (*pronounced* **feert**) *adjective* afraid: *Away hame if ye're feart.*

feartie (*pronounced* **feer**-tee) *noun* a coward: *He wouldnae go on the roller-coaster. He's a right big feartie, isn't he?*

ferntickle (*pronounced* **fern**-tik-l) or **fernietickle** (*pronounced* **fern**-ee-tik-l) *noun* a freckle: *Aw, the wean's cute wee face is covered in fernietickles!* [from the old belief that freckles were the result of being touched or tickled by a fern]

ficher (*pronounced* **fiCH**-er) *verb spoken in Northeast* to fumble or fiddle with something: *There's nae point in ficherin aboot wi' it.*

ficherie (*pronounced* **fiCH**-er-ree) *adjective spoken in Northeast* awkward, fiddly or bothersome: *That's ower ficherie a job for me.*

fiddler's biddin' *noun* a last-minute invitation to some social occasion, such as might be issued to a violin player who will provide the entertainment: *She said she was too proud to go to the wedding on such a fiddler's biddin'.*

finnan haddie *or* **haddock** *noun* a smoked haddock: *It's years since I had a finnan haddie for my breakfast.* [from a local pronunciation of **Findon**, a village south of Aberdeen]

fit *noun* a foot: *The line was nine fit lang.* The saying *a gaun fit's aye gettin* means the active and industrious are the ones who will make the most profit or progress | *pronoun spoken in Northeast & North* what: *Ye ken fine fit Ah mean.*

> This is an example of the Northeast tendency to pronounce the 'wh-' sound as 'f-'. In this way the question *fit like?* means 'how are you?'

fitba (*pronounced* fit-baw) *noun spoken in Glasgow area* football: *Ye cannae call that big numpty a fitba player.*

> Other regions have their own dialect forms of the word, such as *fittie* and *futtie*

fleg *verb* to frighten: *Dinna fleg the bairns wi' yer daft stories.* | *noun* a fright or scare: *Ah got such a fleg when the doorbell went!*

fley (*pronounced* **flay**) *verb* to frighten or scare: *I'll soon fley the likes o' them awa'.*

flype *verb* to turn something inside out: *She sat by the fire flyping socks and darning them.*

flyte *verb* to scold or complain bitterly at someone: *It's no use flyting at one another.* | *noun* (also *flyting*) a dispute or argument: *Whit's a' the flyte aboot?*

> Historically, *flyting* was a competition between
> two poets to decide which could write the most
> wittily abusive verse about the other.

foo *adverb spoken in Northeast* how: *Foo are ye daein'?*

footer *or* **fouter** *verb* to potter or fiddle: *She's footering about in the garden I think.* | *noun* **1** a person who footers: *Will ye leave that phone alone, ye wee footer!* **2** an awkward or fiddly task: *It's a bit of a footer to get those wee screws back in.*

footery *or* **fouterie** *adjective* awkward or fiddly: *Ah havenae the patience for footery wee jobs like that.*

forby *or* **forbye** (*pronounced* for-**bie**) *preposition, adverb* **1** besides or in addition: *There's enough for everybody and more forby.* **2** except: *The whole lot's here, forby one or two.*

forfochen (*pronounced* for-**foCH**-en) *or* **forfochtin** (*pronounced* for-**foCH**-tin) *adjective* exhausted or worn out: *By the end of the open day we were fair forfochen and glad to get home.*

forkietail *noun* an earwig (sometimes shortened to *forkie*): *She found a wee forkietail underneath the sheets in the press.*

fornenst (*pronounced* for-**nenst**) *preposition* situated against or in front of something: *The hoose sat richt fornenst the burn.*

fou *or* **fu'** (*pronounced* **foo**) *adjective* **1** full: *He never halted till the bunker was fou o' coal.* **2** drunk: *Dinnae serve Lachlan ony mair, he's fou.*

Furry Boots City *noun* a nickname for the city of Aberdeen: *We've had a request for Andy Stewart from a listener up in Furry Boots City.*

> One of the distinctive dialect features in
> the Aberdeen area is pronouncing the 'wh-'

sound as 'f-'. In this way, someone asked
by an Aberdonian 'Whereabouts do you
come from?' would hear something like
'fauraeboots …'. The fact that the area is
not known for balmy temperatures also
helps.

fykie (*pronounced* **fie**-ki) *adjective* involving a lot of delicate or
intricate work: *a fykie task*

gads *interjection* a mild expression of disgust or dismay: *Gads!*
Would that no sicken ye? [a euphemistic form of **God**]

gallus (*pronounced* **gal**-luss) *adjective* **1** self-confident,
daring, and often slightly cheeky or reckless: *He's too gallus*
to be intimidated by anyone. **2** *spoken in Glasgow* stylish
or impressive: *Have you seen Davie's new guitar? It's gallus!*
[originally a disapproving term, meaning wild, rascally, and
deserving to be hanged from a **gallows**]

galshachs (*pronounced* **gal**-shaCHs) *plural noun spoken in*
Northeast sweets, cakes, sweet biscuits, and other sweet but not
necessarily healthy delicacies: *empire biscuits, cream buns, an*
suchlike galshachs [perhaps related to the Scots **gulsoch** jaundice
or any sickness caused by over-eating]

gang *verb* to go: *The best laid schemes o' mice and men gang aft*
agley. (*BURNS*)

This is now rather old-fashioned or literary, but
still recognized by most people through being
very common in folk songs and poems.

gawkie (*pronounced* **gaw**-kee) *noun* a person who looks stupid,
clumsy, or awkward: *Who's yon gawkie clackin wi' yer wee sister?*

gawkit (*pronounced* **gaw**-kit) *adjective* stupid, clumsy, or awkward-looking: *a gawkit teenager*

gean (*pronounced* **geen**) *noun* a wild cherry tree or its fruit: *a' thae roses an geans will turn tae bloom* [Old French *guigne*]

geet (*pronounced* **geet**) *noun* spoken in Northeast a child, especially an obnoxious or illegitimate one: *a hoor's geet* [a local variant of *get* and *git*]

geggie (*pronounced* **geg**-ee) *noun* spoken in Glasgow area **1** the mouth, most often heard in the command: *Shut your geggie!* **2** a child's homemade vehicle constructed from pram wheels, wooden boxes, etc: *fleein doon the brae in a geggie*

> It is now very rare to see a child with a homemade vehicle, in these days of skateboards and trainers with wheels in the heel, but the word will still be found in nostalgic contexts.

gey (*pronounced* **gie** or **gay**) *adverb* very or exceptionally: *gey few; It's gey warm in here.*

gillie or **ghillie** (*pronounced* **gil**-ee) *noun* a person employed to act as a guide and assistant to people who are out angling or shooting: *Her father worked as a gillie on an estate in Perthshire.* [Gaelic *gille* a lad or servant]

gimmer *noun* a young ewe between its first and second shearing: *He'd a substantial number of lambs, gimmers, and ewes.* [Old Norse *gymbr* a female lamb]

ging *verb* spoken in Northeast to go: *They're just a pack o' sheep, wi'oot the guts to ging aff on their own.*

girn *verb* to moan, complain, or grumble: *The losers were still girning and whining about the alleged injustice they had suffered.*

glaikit or **glaiket** (*pronounced* **glay**-kit) *adjective* silly, foolish, or thoughtless: *Go and get the mop, you glaikit lump!*; *That's a glaikit way of doing it.*

glaur (*pronounced* **glowr**) *noun* soft, sticky mud: *We were up to our ankles in glaur.*

golach (*pronounced* **gol**-aCH) *noun spoken in East* a beetle: *A muckle great golach came crawlin oot frae under the stane.* [from the Gaelic *gobhlag* an earwig or forked object]

goonie *noun* a nightie or other kind of gown, such as one worn by a patient going to the operating theatre in hospital: *Ah hate these goonies they gie ye in hospital that cannae close up the back.*

gowan (*pronounced* **gow**-an) *noun* a daisy or, occasionally, another similar white or yellow flower: *We twa hae run about the braes, And pou'd the gowans fine.* (BURNS)

gowf (*pronounced* **gowf**) *noun* golf: *The match will take place at Loudoun Gowf Club in Galston.*

> This is slightly old-fashioned, but people still use the word jocularly and it appears in the official name of some golf clubs.

gowfer *noun* a golfer: *A mad keen gowfer will play in any weather.*

gowk (*pronounced* **gowk**) *noun* **1** a cuckoo: *a gowk's nest* **2** a fool or simpleton: *What are you waiting for, you daft gowk?* [Old Norse *gaukr*]

> In some parts of Eastern Scotland, the victim of an April Fool's Day trick is known as an **April gowk**.

graith (*pronounced* **greth**) *noun* equipment, tools, or gear needed for a task: *fishing graith; Hurry up and get the graith into the van.*

gravit (*pronounced* **grah**-vit *or* **graw**-vit) *noun* spoken in Northeast a scarf, especially a warm woollen one: *He had a big red gravit roon his thrapple.* [from **cravat**]

greet *verb* to cry or weep: *What's the wean greetin for?* (The past tense is *grat* and the past participle is *grutten*) | *noun* a period of time spent crying: *I like a good greet at the pictures now and again.* **Greetin face** is a name often applied to someone who always looks miserable: *I see Greetin face was moaning about the referee again.* A **Greetin Teenie** is a person who is always complaining: *Nothing's good enough for the old Greetin Teenie.*

grippie *adjective* spoken in Northeast mean or miserly: *Dinnae expect a tip frae yon grippie auld deil.*

> Northeast Scotland is popularly regarded as having more than its fair share of skinflints, and so it is not surprising that its vocabulary should be well stocked with words such as this.

grosset *noun* a gooseberry: *My grannie used to make grosset wine and bramble jelly.* [from French **groseille**]

grue (*pronounced* **groo**) *verb* to shudder or shiver from fear or disgust: *The taste of that medicine would make ye grue.* Something which **gars ye grue** is so frightening or horrific that it makes your blood run cold

guddle *noun* an untidy or messy place or state: *He's left all my papers in a right guddle.* | *verb* to try to catch a fish from a river or pond with your bare hands: *Two boys were lying on the bank with their hands in the water, obviously guddling for trout.*

gushet (*pronounced* **gush**-it) *noun* a triangular piece of land, such as one between two roads which meet at a sharp angle: *There's a bus stop at the gushet over there.*

gutties *plural noun spoken in West Central & Southwest* plimsolls or trainers: *The boy's needin a new pair o' gutties for gym.* [from **gutta-percha**, a type of rubber used to make soles]

gweed *spoken in Northeast adjective* good: *She gied the press ablow the sink a gweed redd up.* | *noun* a euphemism for God: *Gweed kens fa did it.*

gype (*pronounced* **gipe**) *noun spoken in Northeast* a foolish or stupid person: *He's a glaikit gype.*

haaf (*pronounced* **haf**) *noun spoken in Orkney & Shetland* the open sea, as distinct from coastal waters: *haaf fishing*

haar (*pronounced* **har**) *noun* a cold mist or fog from the North Sea which frequently occurs along the East coast: *The east-coast haar has lowered temperatures in Edinburgh in the morning and evening recently.* [Dutch]

habble *noun* **1** a clumsy, not particularly successful, attempt to do something: *He was having a habble trying to get the childproof lid off the bottle.* **2** a mess: *You've made a right habble of that bedroom.*

hackit *or* **hacket** (*pronounced* **hak**-it) *adjective* ugly, definitely not good-looking: *I do not fancy her. She's hackit!*

haddie *noun* **1** a haddock: *a braw haddie for my tea* **2** a clumsy or silly person: *The car's steering is so good that you have to be a real haddie to get it to misbehave.*

haet (*pronounced* **hayt**) *noun* the smallest amount possible, a whit or iota: *not a haet of difference* [a shortening of the phrase ***deil hae it*** devil have it]

hain (*pronounced* **hayn**) *verb spoken in Northeast* to save something for possible future use: *He's haint aa the pokes he got fae the supermairket.* [from Old Norse **hegna** to hedge or protect]

hallirackit (*pronounced* hal-lee-**rak**-it) *adjective spoken in Northeast* wild, rowdy and irresponsible: *She's a damned hallirackit bitch.* [from Old Scots **halok** a silly thoughtless girl]

hamefare (*pronounced* **haym**-fair) *noun spoken in Orkney & Shetland* the occasion of a newly married woman moving into her new house and the subsequent party celebrating this: *Martha's hamefare became so famous that a song was written about it.*

hap *verb* to cover or wrap: *distant hills happed in mist* To **hap up** means to wrap up or dress warmly for cold weather: *well happed up against the cold* | *noun* a protective covering, such as a heavy coat: *That's a good warm hap you've got there.*

harl *verb* to cover the outside walls of a building with a mixture of lime and gravel or small stones; to roughcast them: *a small development of harled council houses* | *noun* the mixture of lime and gravel used in covering walls in this way: *the white Skye marble which, ground into chips, provided the harl finish to houses in the north*

haud (*pronounced* **hawd**) *verb* to hold: *Haud on and Ah'll chum you up the road.* (The past participle is **hudden** or **hauden**) | *noun* a hold: *Wait till Ah get a haud o' him.*

hauf (*pronounced* **hawf**) *adjective* half: *a hauf-loaf* | *noun* a small glass of whisky. Originally this was a measure of half a gill, and a **wee hauf** was a quarter-gill, but both terms are now used more loosely to mean any smallish measure: *There's a* *guy having a fly hauf in the toilets.* A *hauf an a hauf* is a whisky served with a half-pint of beer as a chaser

haver *or* **haiver** (*pronounced* **hay**-ver) *verb* to talk nonsense: *What's he havering about?* | *noun* **havers** is nonsense: *Don't give me your havers!*

heart-roasted (*pronounced* hart-**roe**-stit) *adjective spoken in Glasgow area* greatly tormented, frustrated, or worried: *He's got his aul mother heart-roasted wi' his wild behaviour.*

heedrum-hodrum (*pronounced* hee-drum-**hoe**-drum) *noun* traditional Gaelic singing or music, as disparaged by unappreciative Lowlanders: *Every Hogmanay we're expected to sit through all this heedrum-hodrum on the telly.* [an attempt to imitate the alleged sound of such music]

heehaw (*pronounced* hee-**haw**) *noun spoken in Glasgow* not the slightest bit or nothing at all: *Just you keep yer nose out of this. You know heehaw about it.* [euphemistic rhyming slang for **damn a'**, **bugger a'**, etc]

heid billydackus (*pronounced* bil-ee-**dak**-uss) *or* **heid pilliedacus** (*pronounced* pil-ee-**dak**-uss) *noun spoken in East* a jocular, even derogatory, name for the person in charge of something [possibly from **billy**, an old word for a man or a workmate, plus a mock Latin ending]

heidie (*pronounced* **hee**-di) *noun* **1** an informal name for the head teacher of a school: *the heidie of an Ayrshire secondary school* **2** an act of striking a football with the head: *The first goal was a divin' heidie.* | *verb* to strike a football with one's head: *He heidied it over the bar.*

hems *noun* To **put the hems on** something is to control, restrain or put a stop to it: *The rain put the hems on our trip to the seaside.*

To **put the hems on** someone is to make them behave in a more restrained or moderate way: *She used to go out with her pals every night, but having that wean's really put the hems on her.* [a **hem** or **haim** was part of the collar put on a working horse]

heuchter-teuchter (*pronounced* hooCH-ter-**chooCH**-ter) *adjective* a derogatory description of Scottish folk and country dance music: *Every time I turn on the radio it's that heuchter-teuchter rubbish.* [probably from a duplication of **teuchter** a mildly derogatory word for a Highlander]

Hielan (*pronounced* **heel**-an) *adjective* **1** Highland: *Munro's much-loved stories about a daft Hielan skipper and a crabbit engineer.* **2** naive, gullible or a bit stupid: *That's a Hielan way of doing things; Ye'll no fool me. I'm no sae Hielan.*

high heid yin (*pronounced* hie-**heed**-yin) *noun* a person in a position of power or authority: *politicians, journalists and academics – opinion-shaping high heid yins in general*

hine or **hine awa** *adverb spoken in Northeast* far away: *hine ayont the braes; They'll be hine awa.*

hin-end (*pronounced* hin-**end** or hin-**en**) *noun* **1** the back, rear, or last section of something: *I might've known you'd turn up at the hin-end o' the day.* **2** a person's backside: *You might tidy up your stuff instead of leaving it all at your hin-end.*

hingy (*pronounced* **hing**-i) *adjective* slightly unwell and looking for sympathy or attention: *Jordan's been a bit hingy all day.* [from the idea of a sick child hanging on to a parent]

hirple *verb* to limp: *He hirpled off injured midway through the second half.* | *noun* a limp: *She's still walking with a bit of a hirple.*

hoatching *adjective* very busy, crowded, or full of something:

Largs is always hoatching on a holiday Monday; The island was hoatching with midges.

hochmagandy *or* **houghmagandie** (*pronounced* hoCH-ma-**gan**-dee) *noun* a jocular or poetic word for sexual intercourse outside marriage: *I wouldnae be surprised if there was a wee bit o' hochmagandy gaun on there.*

Hogmanay (*pronounced* hog-ma-**nay** *or* hug-ma-**nay**) *noun* the 31st of December, New Year's Eve [ultimately from Old French *aguillanneuf* a New Year's Eve gift]

hoolet (*pronounced* **hoo**-lit) *noun* an owl: *woods haunted by the hoolet's cry* [French *hulotte* an owl]

hoor *noun* **1** literally, a prostitute; but the word is often used as an offensive term for any woman: *He's running around wi' some wee hoor fae Fife; Shut up, ye auld hoor!* **2** any unpleasant person or thing: *We'd a hoor o' a job gettin it clean.* [Scots form of **whore**]

hoose (*pronounced* **hooss**) *noun* a house: *Come ben the hoose.*

horny-golach (*pronounced* hor-nee-**gol**-aCH) *noun* spoken in Northeast an earwig: *It's only an earwig, what my grannie used to call a horny-golach.* [see **golach**]

hough (*pronounced* **hawCH**) *noun* a joint of meat cut from the shin of the pig or cow: *Fling a ham hough intae the soup tae gie it flavour.* [Old English *hōh* meaning heel]

howe (*pronounced* **how**) *noun* a depression or hollow in the landscape, an area of low-lying land surrounded by hills (sometimes used in place names): *the Howe of Fife*

howff (*pronounced* **howf**) *noun* a place, especially a pub, used as a regular meeting place: *a lively musical howff with excellent real ale* [probably Dutch or Flemish *hof* a courtyard or enclosed space]

howk (*pronounced* **howk**) *verb* to extract something by, or as if by, digging or scraping: *We saw a few locals exercising their right to howk for cockles by hand and bucket; ballads howked from a spare and hostile landscape* [from old Low German]

howtowdie (*pronounced* how-**tow**-dee) *noun* a dish of boiled chicken with spinach and poached eggs: *Chicken forms the basis of both cock-a-leekie and howtowdie.* [from Old French *hétoudeau* or *estaudeau* a fat young chicken for cooking]

huckle *verb spoken in Glasgow* to force someone to move by manhandling them or bundling them roughly: *I huckled her out the door before she could say anything else.*

hudderie (*pronounced* **hud**-er-i) *adjective* untidy or scruffy: *Yer hair's awfy hudderie lookin, is it no?*

humph *verb* to carry something heavy: *The main problem with living in a top flat is having to humph your messages up three flights of stairs.*

hurdies *plural noun* the buttocks and hips

hurl *noun* a lift or journey in a car or other motor vehicle: *Any chance of a hurl into town?*

hyter (*pronounced* **hie**-ter) *verb spoken in Northeast* to stumble or lurch: *He went hyterin aff tae his bed.*

ill-trickit (*pronounced* il-**trik**-it) *adjective spoken in Northeast* naughty or mischievous: *an ill-trickit bairn*

ingin or **ingan** (*pronounced* **ing**-in) *noun* an onion: *See's two pun o' ingins.*

intimmers (*pronounced* in-**tim**-merz) *plural noun spoken in Northeast* the insides, of practically anything from the internal workings of a clock to a person's stomach and intestines: *Ah*

27

doot there's somethin' no quite right in ma intimmers. [originally the internal **timbers** of a ship's hull]

jag *verb* to prick something: *He jagged his hand on the barbed wire.* | *noun* an instance of being pricked or, most usually, a jab or injection: *The wean got a jag at school the day.*

jaggy *adjective* prickly or pointed: *There's something jaggy in my shoe.* | *noun* a stinging nettle: *She fell in the jaggies and ran hame greetin.*

jalouse (*pronounced* ja-**looz**) *verb* to suspect or infer: *I jaloused ye'd be wantin yer tea.*

jannie *noun* a school janitor or caretaker: *Run and ask the jannie for the spare key.*

jaup (*pronounced* **jop**) *verb* to splash or spatter: *His breeks were a' jaupit wi mud fae the fields.* | *noun* a splash or spilt drop: *Don't get jaups of paint on my good carpet.*

jawbox *noun* a kitchen sink: *Ye'll get Vim and a cloth in ablow the jawbox.* [perhaps from the Scots **jaw** meaning to splash or pour]

jenny-a'-things (*pronounced* jen-nee-**aw**-thingz) *noun* a small shop selling a wide variety of goods: *Awa' an' see if the jenny-a'-things is open yet.*

> The term literally refers to an establishment run by a woman and selling everything you could desire.

jenny longlegs *noun* a crane fly: *Daddy, there's a big jenny longlegs in my bedroom.*

jessie *noun* an effeminate, weak, or cowardly man: *What are ye greetin for, ye big jessie?; Shinty is not a game for jessies.*

It is not clear why this particular girls' name was chosen for this use, or indeed whether Scottish women called Jessie were historically any feebler than your average Mary or Margaret.

jing-bang (*pronounced* jing-**bang**) *noun* the whole lot or everything: *Ah'm scunnered wi' the hale jing-bang o' them.*

jings *interjection* an exclamation of mild surprise: *Jings! I didn't know we weren't supposed to sit here.*

This exclamation might not have become so common had it not been immortalized by Scotland's most famous cartoon family, The Broons.

jink *verb* to move swiftly or jerkily or make a quick turn in order to dodge: *He jinked through from 20 metres out for a superb individual try.*

jouk (*pronounced* **jook**) *verb* to duck or dodge: *She jouked out the way of the snowball.* | *noun* a sudden evasive movement: *With a sudden jouk up a close the cat left her pursuers behind.*

keech (*pronounced* **keeCH**) *noun* excrement: *Ah've gone and stood on a dog's keech.*

keelie (*pronounced* **keel**-i) *noun* a young working-class person from a city or large town, especially Glasgow: *She married a right Glesca keelie.* [from Gaelic **gille** a lad]

You have to be careful in using this term. To many people it is derogatory and will be taken as an insult implying being rough and uncultured. On the other hand, some individuals, particularly Glaswegians, will proudly describe themselves as keelies.

kenspeckle *adjective* familiar, well-known, or easily recognized: *He is a kenspeckle figure in Edinburgh's Asian community.* [perhaps from Old Norse **kennispecki** power of recognition]

kist *noun* a large chest or wooden box: *This is the kist where they used to keep sheets and blankets.*

kittle *or* **kittlie** *adjective* unpredictable and capricious: *He's aye been kittle tae deal wi'.* | *verb* **1** to be puzzling or troubling to someone: *That's something that kittles me yet.* **2** to tickle or be ticklish: *Stop kittlin the weans or they'll never go down the night.*

knowe *or* **know** (*pronounced* **now**) *noun* a small rounded hill: *Ca' the yowes tae the knowes.* [a Scots form of **knoll**]

knype on (*pronounced* **nipe**) *verb spoken in Northeast* to keep going or slog away at something, often used in the sense of going steadily through life without any great mishap: *Aye knypin on?* [**Knype** literally means to knock]

kye *plural noun* cattle: *The kye are in the byre.*

lade *noun* a watercourse, especially one that carries water to a mill: *The old mill lade off the River Leithen powered five woollen mills and a saw-mill.*

laich *or* **laigh** (*pronounced* **layCH**) *adjective* low: *a laich whisper*

laird *noun* a lord, especially the owner of a large estate: *a sixteenth-century laird's mansion*

laldie *or* **laldy** (*pronounced* **lal**-dee) *noun* To **give it laldie** means to do something vigorously: *Down one end of the room there was a gang of folkies giving it laldy, and good foot-tapping music filled the bar.*

laverock (*pronounced* **lav**-er-ok *or* **layv**-rok) *noun* a skylark (the bird): *We could hear a laverock singing somewhere high above.*

law *noun spoken in Lowlands* a hill, especially a rounded one (often used as part of a place name): *Broad Law; Dundee Law* | *adjective* low: *the law, law lands o' Holland*

leet *noun* a list of candidates for a job, award, contract, etc: *She was on the short leet of four applicants interviewed on May 21.*

leid (*pronounced* **leed**) *noun* a chiefly literary word for a language: *the auld Scots leid* [Old English]

linn *noun* a waterfall or the pool at the foot of one: *A couple of anglers were trying their luck on the linn.* [from the Gaelic **linne** a pool and the Old English **hlynn** a torrent]

lintie *noun* a linnet: *singin like a lintie*

lippen *verb* to trust or depend on: *Ye maunna lippen til him.*

loon *or* **loun** *noun spoken in Northeast* a boy or lad: *He was a local loon, born and bred in Aberdeen.*

> It is worth noting that in Northest Scotland calling someone a loon does not indicate that you think they are a fool - at least, not necessarily.

loup *or* **lowp** (*pronounced* **lowp**) *verb* to leap or jump: *If you wait long enough, you might see a salmon louping.* | *noun* a leap or jump: *He cleared the dyke with one great loup.*

lowse (*pronounced* **lowss**) *adjective* loose: *Is this skirt no a bit lowse?* | *verb* **1** to loose or release something: *Doon she lowsed her bonny black hair.* **2** to finish work: *They lowse at five o'clock.* **Lowsin time** is the time at which work or school finishes: *I'll get ye at the gate at lowsin time.*

lum *noun* a chimney: *Run next door and tell them their lum's on fire!* The traditional saying **lang may your lum reek** (literally, long may your chimney smoke) is a way of wishing someone long life and prosperity

machair (*pronounced* **maCH**-er) *noun* a type of low-lying sandy grassy land found just above the high-water mark of many sandy shores in western Scotland, particularly in the Hebrides. It is often more fertile than the more mountainous areas further inland: *unspoilt miles of machair, beach, and headland* [Gaelic]

> Machair is such a distinctive element of Hebridean life that the word was used as the title of a Gaelic-language soap opera set on the Isle of Lewis, first broadcast on Scottish Television in the 1990s.

maddie *noun* a wild or crazy person: *Tell that maddie tae stop shoutin an bawlin.*

makar (*pronounced* **mak**-er) *noun* a poet: *a grand meetin o' a' the makars*

> While this is chiefly an old-fashioned or literary word, it was used as recently as 2004 when Edwin Morgan was named as the first Scots Makar, or national poet of Scotland.

malky (*pronounced* **mal**-kee) *spoken in Glasgow noun* a slang term for a razor used as a weapon: *She used to take his malky into the dancehall for him in her handbag.* | *verb* to slash someone with a razor: *A boy got malkied in there last night.*

> Apparently this comes from rhyming slang for Malcolm Fraser, but the identity of this individual has been lost in the mists of time and

booze. He is certainly not to be identified with
the former Australian prime minister of that
name.

mannie *noun* **1** any man: *the mannie from the gas board* **2**
spoken in Northeast the man in charge of something, especially
if he is also its owner, for instance a farmer or the skipper of a
fishing boat

mappie-mou (*pronounced* map-ee-**moo**) *noun spoken in
Northeast* the antirrhinum or snapdragon: *a braw display o'
mappie-mous in the front gairden* [from **mappie**, a pet name for a
rabbit, plus **mou** mouth]

maun (*pronounced* **mawn**) *verb* must: *He maun hae dropped it.*

mawkit *adjective spoken in West Central* **1** very dirty: *a mawkit
semmit* **2** offensively bad: *That singing's mawkit!* [literally,
infested with maggots, from **mauk**, an old Scots name for a
maggot]

meen *noun spoken in Northeast* the moon: *Oot frae the clouds
came the bonnie meen.*

meenit *noun* a minute: *It's only five meenits tae lowsin time.*

meggy-mony-feet (*pronounced* meg-ee-**mun**-nee-feet) *noun*
a centipede

meikle (*pronounced* **meek**-il) *adjective* big or large (often found
in place names): *Meikle Earnock*

meiny (*pronounced* **may**-nee) *noun spoken in Northeast* a
disparaging word for a crowd or large group of people; a rabble:
amang the meiny in Union Street [from Old French]

merse (*pronounced* **merss**) *noun spoken in South* an area of
low-lying fertile land near a river or shore: *the peaceful sight*

of cattle grazing on the merse **The Merse** is a low-lying fertile region in the Eastern Borders, between the River Tweed and the Lammermuir Hills [Old English, meaning marsh]

messan (*pronounced* **mess**-an) *noun spoken in Central & South* an obnoxious or contemptible person: *Stop that right now, ye dirty wee messan!* [ultimately from Gaelic *measan* meaning small dog]

midden *noun* **1** the area at the back of a block of flats where the communal dustbins are kept: *Ye cannae stop weans playin in the midden.* **2** a dunghill: *the reek o' the midden by the byre* **3** any dirty or untidy person or thing: *Are you ever going to clean this place up, ye dirty auld midden?*; *This room's a right midden.*

midgie (*pronounced* **mij**-ee) *noun* **1** a midge: *The midgies were out in force and we soon retreated indoors.* **2** a dustbin or litter bin: *An old tramp was raking through the midgies.* [sense 2 comes from the word *midden*]

ming *verb* to smell strongly and unpleasantly: *It's great to be able to go to the pub and not come home minging of cigarette smoke.* | *noun* a strong unpleasant smell or stink: *There's a right ming coming from the fridge.*

mink *or* **minker** *noun spoken in East* a scruffy or disreputable person: *He's away oot dressed lik a minker.* [from Gaelic *muince* a collar, figuratively used to mean a noose and implying that the person referred to would be, to quote the 19th-century judge Lord Braxfield, "nane the waur o' a hanging"]

minky *adjective spoken in East* dirty or disgusting: *Have you no cleaned those minky shoes yet?*; *Having to go out begging made me feel all minky.*

mixter-maxter (*pronounced* mik-ster-**mak**-ster) *or* **mixtie-**

maxtie *adjective, adverb* in an untidy jumbled way: *Papers were strewn mixter-maxter across the desk.* | *noun* a confused jumble: *The film contains a mixter-maxter of inadequately thought out ideas.*

mochie or **mochy** (*pronounced* moCH-ee) *adjective* damp, misty, and unpleasantly humid: *It's awfy mochie weather we hae the noo.* [from Old Norse *mugga* mist]

mollach (*pronounced* mol-aCH) *verb spoken in Northeast* to hang around or wander about aimlessly: *Fit are ye mollachin aboot at?* [from the behaviour of *moles*, in throwing up molehills apparently at random]

moothie *noun* a mouth-organ or harmonica: *He's one of the best moothie players in all Scotland.*

mowdie or **mowdiewart** (*pronounced* mow-dee-wort) *noun* a mole (the animal): *I see the mowdies have been busy in your back garden.* [from *moldewarpe*, literally earth-thrower, an archaic name for a mole]

nabbler *noun spoken in Northeast* a fast and skilful worker: *Ye can mak guid money, gin ye're a nabbler.*

nae (*pronounced* nay) *adjective* no or not: *There's nae mair; She'll nae be back yet.*

nash *verb spoken in Edinburgh area* to hurry or dash: *I'll just nash along to the shop for a paper.* [Romany]

ned *noun spoken in Glasgow area* a young male hooligan or petty criminal: *He's a right wee ned.* [shortened from Edward, perhaps related to teddy boy]

nedette (*pronounced* ned-**et**) *noun spoken in Glasgow area* a female ned: *nedettes in their muffin tops*

neep *noun* a turnip: *The farmhands are lifting neeps.*

Ne'erday (*pronounced* **nair**-day) *noun* New Year's Day: *the Ne'erday television highlights*

neuk (*pronounced* **nyook**) *noun* **1** a corner or nook: *sitting in a neuk by the fire* **2** an area of land that projects into the sea: *the East Neuk of Fife*

numpty *noun* *spoken in Glasgow area* a stupid person: *That's no the way to do it, ya numpty!*

nyaff (*pronounced* n-**yaff**) *noun* a worthless or irritating person, especially a small one: *Never mind what that wee nyaff says.* [perhaps an imitation of the barking of a small dog]

oose (*pronounced* **ooss**) *noun* dust or fluff: *Have you seen the oose under that bed?* [originally the plural of *oo*, a Scots word for wool]

orra (*pronounced* **or**-ra or **or**-ree) *adjective* *spoken in Tayside & Northeast* coarse or uncouth in behaviour or speech: *When she talks like that we feel all orra and common.* On a traditional Scottish farm, an **orraman**, **orra lad**, or (in the Northeast) **orra loon** was a man or boy employed to do miscellaneous unskilled work: *Leave that til the orraman.* [perhaps from *ower a'* over all, everywhere or general]

ower (*pronounced* **ow**-er) *preposition* over: *He flung it ower the wa'.* | *adverb* too or excessively: *It's ower warm for a jumper.*

owergyaan (*pronounced* owr-**gyahn**) *or* **owergan** (*pronounced* owr-**gan**) *noun* *spoken in Northeast* a scolding or telling-off: *a gweed owergyaan* [Compare the English *going-over*, a scolding or thrashing]

oxter *noun* an armpit: *Ah'm up tae ma oxters in work the noo.*

pap *verb* to throw: *Pap that in the bucket, will you?; He got* *papped out of the Uni after failing his resits.* | *noun* **1** a female breast: *a bairn at the pap* **2** used in the name of various conical, roughly breast-shaped, hills: *the Paps of Jura*

partan (*pronounced* **par**-tan) *noun* a crab, especially a common edible crab, often made into a soup called **partan bree**: *There was no lobster in the creel, only a couple of partans.* [Gaelic]

pawkie or **pawky** (*pronounced* **paw**-ki) *adjective* showing a dry sense of humour, especially when a shrewd and down-to-earth criticism of hypocrisy or pretension is involved: *learned enthusiasm sprinkled with a pawky sense of humour* [from the earlier **pawk** a trick]

pech (*pronounced* **peCH**) *verb* to pant for breath, especially after exerting yourself: *We were all peching by the time we reached the top.* **peched out** means exhausted and out of breath: *I was that peched out I had to sit down.*

peedie *adjective spoken in Orkney & Caithness* small: *just a peedie boy*

peely-wally or **peelie-wallie** (*pronounced* pee-lee-**wal**-lee) *adjective* **1** pale and unhealthy-looking: *She says she's fine but she looks peely-wally to me.* **2** lacking in the desired strength or vigour: *This tea's a bit peely-wally.*

peenge *verb* to moan or complain in a whining, peevish manner: *Stop your peengeing, we've only got a little further to go.*

peerie heels *plural noun spoken in Central & South* stiletto heels: *peerie heels and pointed toes* [from **peerie** meaning small]

perjink (*pronounced* per-**jink**) *adjective* neat and precise about things to the point of being fussy or prim: *She's awful perjink about her appearance.*

photie *noun* a photograph: *Staun ower there till I take yer photie.*

piece *noun* a sandwich or slice of bread eaten as part of a packed lunch or as a snack: *We sat on a bench to eat our pieces; a piece and cheese*

pinkie *noun* the little finger: *I'm practising drinking coffee with my pinkie in the air.* [from Dutch **pink** little finger]

plank *verb* **1** to put something away somewhere safe or hidden for later use: *The old man's got a few cans planked away somewhere.* **2** to place or put something down in a forceful manner: *He planked the file down on the desk in front of me.* | *noun* a secret supply or cache of something: *His mum found a plank of jazz mags under his bed.*

playpiece *noun* any snack, such as a biscuit, a packet of crisps, or an apple, that a child takes to school to eat during the morning break or interval: *The wean's away tae school withoot her playpiece.*

plettie *noun spoken in Dundee* a balcony or landing in a block of flats: *sittin oot on the plettie drinkin a can ae export* [from **plat** meaning flat or level]

plook or **plouk** *noun* a pimple: *That's him there, the wan wi' plooks a' ower his face.*

plooky or **plookit** *adjective* having a lot of pimples: *I'm too plooky to go out the night.*

plouter (*pronounced* **plow**-ter) *verb* to splash through, or play about with, water or mud: *The bairns were havin' a rare time plowterin' through the puddles.*

plump *noun* a sudden, heavy fall of rain: *Take your brolly; there's* *going to be a plump.*

pochle or **pauchle** (*pronounced* **poCH**-l) *verb* to dishonestly rig or fix something so that a particular result is obtained: *He is widely believed to be the man who pochled the election; To some people it is "creative accountancy", to others it is simply pochling the books.* | *noun* an instance of cheating; a swindle or fiddle: *The chairman's wife won first prize in the raffle: talk about a pochle!* [from the Old Scots **pakkald**, ultimately from **pack** a bundle]

pook *noun* a tuft of hair, wool, etc. sticking out from something: *There's a pook on your jumper.*

port-a-beul (*pronounced* **porsh**-ta-**bee**-al) *noun* the singing of simple or meaningless words to a tune originally intended as purely instrumental music: *He won a medal at the Mod for his port-a-beul.* [Gaelic, meaning music from mouth]

prig *verb spoken in North* to beg, plead, or beseech: *It had taken a lot of prigging to get her to go.*

prog *verb* to pierce or prick something, or to stick something pointed into it: *I always prog the ham with cloves before cooking it.*

puddock *noun* a frog or toad: *She found a wee orange puddock in the back garden.* [from Old English **pad** a toad]

puggy or **puggie** *noun* **1** a fruit machine or one-armed bandit: *He lost all his cash on the puggy.* **2** a cash-dispenser machine: *Sorry I took so long; there was some queue at the puggy.* **3** an old name for a monkey: *Anybody ever tell ye ye've got a face like a puggie?* The saying **fou as a puggie** means very drunk. To **get your puggie up** or **take a puggie** means to lose one's temper: *He took a puggie an flung his mobile oot the windae.*

purvey (*pronounced* **per**-vee) *noun* the food and drink provided after a funeral, at a wedding reception, etc.: *There'll be a bit of* *a purvey at the Miners' Welfare afterwards.* [from Old French **porveeir** to provide]

quaich (*pronounced* **kwayCH**) *noun* a small shallow drinking cup, usually with two handles, nowadays mostly used as ornaments or trophies: *He gave his best man a fine silver quaich.* [Gaelic **cuach** cup]

queenie *noun* a type of shellfish (a queen scallop): *a stew of squid, queenies, monkfish, and crab*

queet *noun spoken in Northeast* an ankle: *She strained her queet.* [from older Scots **cuit**, which comes from Middle Dutch]

quine (*pronounced* **kwine**) or **quean** (*pronounced* **kween**) *noun spoken in Northeast* a young unmarried woman or girl: *He had mairrit on a quine fae Torry.* [Old English]

radge or **raj** or **radgie** or **rajie** *spoken in Edinburgh & East adjective* To be or go **radge** is to act in a wild or crazy way: *He went totally radge when he heard what I'd done.* | *noun* someone who behaves in a wild or irrational way: *D'ye ken whit the radge did next?* [probably a variant of **rage**, although it may be influenced by the Romany **raj** stupid or crazy]

raggle *noun* a groove cut in a piece of stone or wood to enable another piece to fit into it: *This is the raggle that was cut to take the roof.* | *verb* to cut such a groove in a piece of stone or wood: *Raggling the walls makes a real mess.*

raivel (*pronounced* **ray**-vel) *verb* **1** to become tangled or confused: *Dinna let the cat raivel yer knittin'; The fishin' lines are a' raivelt.* **2** to baffle or confuse: *His mind's aa raivelt.*

rammy *noun* a noisy fight or brawl: *Tempers flared, leading to a rammy involving groups of youths from the two towns.*

ramstam (*pronounced* ram-**stam**) *adverb, adjective* in a hurried and clumsy way, without proper care or thought: *She aye goes at it ramstam.*

randan (*pronounced* ran-**dan**) *noun* a spree or a wild or dissolute good time, frequently but not necessarily one involving heavy drinking: *They were out on the randan to celebrate the end of term.* [probably from **random**]

rax *verb* **1** to stretch your body or a part of your body: *He raxed out his arm.* **2** to fetch something or give it to someone else with an outstretched arm: *Rax us ower the salt.* **3** to sprain or wrench a limb by stretching or turning it too far or too energetically: *He's aff work after raxin' his shoulder.* [Old English]

redd *verb* to clear or tidy up something: *I must get round to redding up that cupboard sometime.* | *noun* an act of tidying a place up: *We'll need to give the front room a good redd before your mother comes.*

reese (*pronounced* **reez**) *verb* *spoken in Northeast* to praise or extol: *He aye reesed the wifie's bannocks.*

reestit (*pronounced* **ree**-stit) *adjective* *spoken in Shetland* (referring to food) cured by drying or smoking: *Reestit mutton is a Shetland speciality, a type of wind-dried mutton used for making soup.* [probably Scandinavian]

rickle *noun* a loose heap or pile of things: *The old house was now just a rickle of stones.* To say someone is *a rickle of banes* is a picturesque way of saying that they are unhealthily thin [probably Scandinavian]

rive *verb* to pull or tug something firmly, or to tear it by pulling at it: *We rived at the tree-stump but couldn't shift it.* | *noun* a firm pull or tug: *He gie'd it such a rive that it came awa' in his haun.*

roch (*pronounced* **roCH**) *adjective* rough: *Yon's a gey roch pub.*

ronepipe *or* **rhonepipe** *noun* one of the drain pipes running from the gutter on a roof to the ground: *He was locked out, so he thought he'd climb up the ronepipe.*

roup (*pronounced* **rowp**) *noun* an auction: *They said goods and effects will be sold by public roup.*

rowie *noun* *spoken in Northeast* the type of flaky, butter-rich, bread roll, originally from Aberdeen, which is generally called a **buttery** elsewhere in Scotland: *and half a dozen rowies, please*

rummlethump (*pronounced* **rum**-l-thump) *or* **rummledethump** (*pronounced* **rum**-l-dee-thump) *noun* a dish made of cabbage mixed into mashed potatoes: *wild salmon on a bed of rummledethump*

runkle *verb* to crease or crumple something: *His jacket was all runkled when he took it down from the locker.*

saftie *noun* **1** *spoken in Northeast* a soft bread roll, a bap, as distinct from a **rowie**: *twa safties, twa rowies, and a French stick* **2** slippers are sometimes called *safties*: *The dug's awa' wi' ma safties again!*

sair *adjective* **1** aching and painful: *a sair heid* **2** difficult or requiring a lot of effort: *Aye, it's a sair fecht havin tae work for a livin.*

sannies *plural noun* *spoken in Central* gym-shoes or plimsolls: *Do thae sannies still fit ye?* [shortened from **sandshoes**]

sapple *spoken in Central* *verb* to rinse something or wash it out: *Sapple that teapot till I put the kettle on again.* | *noun* soapy lather: *She plunged another cardie into the sapples.*

scaffie *or* **scaffy** *noun* a street-sweeper or dustman; often used as a term of abuse to imply that someone is dirty: *Ah wouldnae gie that clown a start as a scaffie; Away and put on a clean shirt, ya scaffie!* [shortened from **scavenger**]

scart *verb* to scratch or scrape: *Ah scartit ma heid on a branch.* | *noun* A **scart** is a scratch or scrape: *Oor hauns were a' scarts wi' pickin brambles; a well-fired roll wi' just a wee scart o' butter*

schemie (*pronounced* **skee**-mi) *noun* a person who lives on one of the large council housing estates (schemes) on the outskirts of many Scottish towns: *The bus was full of schemies heading into town for their Saturday night's entertainment.*

sclaff *verb* 1 to hit something, especially a ball, with a glancing blow: *The striker swung his boot at the loose ball but only succeeded in sclaffing it wide for a goal-kick.* 2 in golf, to mishit the ball because the head of the club has hit the ground a glancing blow before striking the ball: *You wouldn't expect a player of her calibre to sclaff an approach shot.* | *noun* a slap or glancing blow, or a golf shot mishit as described above: *The branch swung back and gave him a sclaff on the ear.*

sclim *verb* to climb: *When I was wee I could sclim up that tree no bother.* (The past tense can be either *sclimmed* or *sclam*)

scoosh or **skoosh** *verb* to squirt or spurt: *He scooshed me with a water pistol; Water came scooshing out of the tap.* If you do something easily, without having to make a serious effort you might be said to *scoosh it*: *At home to Stenhousemuir in the next round? Ach, we'll scoosh it.* | *noun* 1 a squirt or spurt of liquid: *Put another wee scoosh of cream on it.* 2 any fizzy soft drink: *Ah could murder a can o' scoosh.* 3 something that is considered very easy to deal with (also *scoosh case*): *Buying a new house in the current market is easy, a scoosh case.*

scud *noun* a slap or smack: *Are you wanting a scud on the lug?*
In the scud or, even more shockingly, **in the bare scud**, means
naked: *She was wandering around the house in the bare scud.*
| *verb* to slap or smack: *I'll scud your ear in a minute.*

scunner *verb* to irritate or disgust: *Behaviour like that
scunners me, so it does.* **scunnered** means sickened or disgusted,
either because something is unpleasant or because you are
utterly fed up with it: *I'm scunnered with having to get up at
six every morning.* | *noun* a feeling of disgust or loathing, or
whatever causes this feeling: *I took a scunner to Shakespeare
when I had to study him at Uni; This weather's a right scunner,
isn't it?*

selt *verb* a Scottish past form of sell, often used instead of sold:
Have ye selt yer hoose yet?

semmit or **simmit** (*pronounced* **sem**-mit *or* **sim**-mit) *noun* a
vest: *No wonder you're cold. Away and put your semmit on.*

sharger (*pronounced* **sharg**-er) *noun spoken in Northeast* a
weak, puny, or stunted-looking person or animal: *Nane o' my
bairns hae been shargers.* [Gaelic *searg* a puny creature]

shargert (*pronounced* **sharg**-ert) or **shargered** (*pronounced*
sharg-erd) *adjective spoken in Northeast* weak, puny, or stunted
looking: *a shargert-lookin' quine*

sharn or **shairn** *noun* dung, especially the dung of cattle:
sharn on his boots

shauchle (*pronounced* **shawCH**-l) *verb* to walk slowly and
awkwardly without lifting your feet properly: *Some old guy was
shauchling along the street.*

sheugh or **sheuch** (*pronounced* **shuCH**) *noun* **1** a gutter or ditch for drainage: *a long sheugh which his father had dug with a pick and shovel* If you are said to be **up a sheugh** or **up the sheugh** you are completely mistaken or have the wrong idea entirely: *Ah doot we're up the sheuch this time.* **2** the entire area around the buttocks and genitals: *He's a wee dumpy guy – always looks as if his sheuch's too near the ground; sweaty sheuch syndrome, as experienced during driving tests* **3** more specifically, the cleft between the buttocks: *I could feel the sweat trickling into the sheuch o' my erse.* [from Middle English **sogh** a swamp]

shilpit (*pronounced* **shil**-pit) *adjective* thin and weak-looking, as if underfed or in poor health: *Who's that wee shilpit-lookin' creature next tae you in the photie?*

shirrackin or **sherrackin** (*pronounced* **sher**-rak-in) *noun spoken in Glasgow* a severe scolding or telling-off: *The weans got a right shirrackin for no sayin' where they were gaun.*

shoogle *verb* to shake, sway, or rock from side to side: *The trailer shoogled alarmingly as we drove up the track; He shoogled his son awake.* | *noun* a shake, push or nudge: *Give me a shoogle if it looks like I'm falling asleep.*

shoogly (*pronounced* **shoo**-gul-i) *adjective* shaky, unsteady or wobbly: *That's an awful shoogly table.* If your **jaicket is on a shoogly nail** or **peg** you are in danger of losing your job: *That's the second big order we've lost this month. The boss's jaicket must be on a shoogly peg.*

shunky *noun* a toilet: *I've just got time tae nip tae the shunky afore we go.*

> The word may possibly come from Shanks & Co of Barrhead, near Glasgow, a well-known manufacturer of ceramic ware whose brand-

name on their goods will have impressed itself
on generations of grateful users.

simmer dim *noun* *spoken in Orkney & Shetland* the night-
long twilight in Orkney and Shetland in midsummer, when
dusk runs more or less directly into dawn and it is never truly
dark: *up all night enjoying the simmer dim*

skail (*pronounced* **skayl**) *verb* **1** if someone says a building, such
as a factory, pub, or hall is *skailing*, it is emptying at the end of a
shift, closing time, etc. You can also say that the occupants are
skailing: *The road's aye busy when the bingo's skailing; We were
held up by the crowd skailin oot o' Murrayfield.* **2** to spill: *Watch
you don't skail my pint!*

skeich (*pronounced* **skeeCH**) *adjective* **1** in an excited, lively but
easily upset mood (often used of young children): *The bairns're
ower skeich already wi'oot yon nonsense.* **2** fit and active: *The old
mannie's as skeich as ony youngster.*

skelf *noun* **1** a splinter of wood, especially one embedded in
your skin: *He was taking a skelf out of his thumb with a pin.* **2** a
small thin person: *What does a wee skelf of a lassie like her need
to diet for?*

skelp *noun* a smack or slap: *All that boy needs is a good skelp.*
| *verb* **1** to smack or slap: *Ah hate tae see a mammy skelpin' her
wean.* **2** to move or go quickly: *He went skelping down the road
after the bus.*

skiddle *verb* to splash or spill water or another liquid or to
play about splashily with water: *bairns skiddlin' in the paddlin'
pool* | *noun* a wet splashed or spilled mess, or a period of time
spent playing about with water: *Mop up that skiddle on the
kitchen floor.*

skinnymalink (*pronounced* **skin**-ee-ma-link) *or*
skinnymalinkie (*pronounced* skin-ee-ma-**link**-ee) *noun* a
jocular name for any very thin person or animal: *Is that boy of
theirs still such a big skinnymalink?*

skirlie *noun* a dish of oatmeal and onions fried together,
eaten either as a vegetable with meat dishes, or on its own with
potatoes: *There's a choice of skirlie or neeps as a side course.*

skite *verb* **1** to slip or slide: *Watch ye don't skite on that icy
pavement.* **2** to bounce rapidly from a surface: *My ball skited
off the green and into the bunker; The hail was skitin' off the
pavement.* | *noun* a glancing blow or slap: *You're askin' for a
skite on the lug.* Someone who is **on the skite** is on a drunken
spree: *staggering home after a night on the skite*

skittery *or* **skitterie** *adjective* fiddly and time-consuming:
It's a skittery job threading a needle.

skliff *or* **scliff** *verb* to walk without lifting your feet properly,
so that your shoes scrape along the ground: *If you don't stop
that scliffing your good shoes'll need soled in no time.* | *noun* **1** the
sound made by someone's shoes scraping along the ground
as they walk: *She could hear the skliff of his boots in the close as
he came wearily up the steps.* **2** a segment of something: *Gie's a
skliff of your orange.*

slàinte mhath (*pronounced* **slan**-ja **vah**) *interjection* a Gaelic
toast used especially when drinking whisky (often shortened to
slàinte) [literally meaning good health]

sleekit (*pronounced* **slee**-kit) *adjective* outwardly charming and
smooth, but actually untrustworthy and sly: *She's a sleekit two-
faced besom.*

sleuch (*pronounced* **sloo**CH) *or* **sluch** (*pronounced* **slu**CH) *verb* to drink noisily, usually from a spoon or through a straw: *Do you have to sleuch your soup like that?*

slitter or **slutter** *spoken in Central & South* *noun* a messy eater or drinker: *You've got pakora sauce all down your front, you slitter!* | *verb* to make a mess, especially by spilling or dribbling something: *Now, I want no sluttering on my good tablecloth.*

slunge *verb* to rinse something superficially by pouring water over it or dipping it into water: *I'll just slunge the mugs out under the tap.*

smeddum (*pronounced* **smed**-dum) *noun* an admirable mixture of determination, resourcefulness and common sense: *I like a lassie wi' a bit o' smeddum.* [Old English *smedema*]

smirr *noun* drizzly rain falling gently in small drops: *a smirr o' rain; There's a bit of a smirr outside.* | *verb* to rain in light drizzle: *It's been smirring all afternoon.*

smowt or **smout** *noun* **1** a small person, whether a child or undersized adult: *Ye're no feart fae that wee smowt?* **2** a young salmon or sea trout: *A smowt like this should be thrown back in.*

snash *noun* cheeky, impudent talk: *Ah'm no takin any snash fae the likes o' her!*

sneck *noun* a catch or latch on a door, gate etc: *Just lift the sneck and go in.* | *verb* to fasten a door, gate etc it with a catch or latch: *The coos'll no get oot if ye sneck the gate efter ye.*

snell *adjective* bitingly cold: *It's a snell wind that's blawin' aff the braes.* [Old English]

snib *noun* a bolt or catch on a door or window: *Put the snib on the front door before you go to bed.* | *verb* to lock a door or window using a snib: *The door'll no open; it must be snibbed on the inside.*

snorl *noun spoken in Northeast* an awkward situation, a scrape or predicament: *Whit a snorl ye've got yersel intil!* [from **snarl**]

sonsie or **sonsy** (*pronounced* **sonss**-ee) *adjective* plump, cheerful-looking, and attractive: *She was a big, braw, sonsie lass.* [Gaelic **sonas** meaning good fortune]

sook or **souk** *verb* to suck: *The wean was sookin' its dummy.* If you **sook in** or **sook up** you are trying to curry favour with someone by behaving sycophantically: *You only get on here if you're prepared to sook in to the boss.* | *noun* **1** a suck: *Gie's a sook o' yer ice lolly.* **2** someone who behaves sycophantically towards their superiors; a crawler or toady: *He sits through every meeting, grinning and nodding like a total sook.*

sooth-moother (*pronounced* sooth-**moodh**-er) *noun spoken in Shetland* someone with an accent from a more southerly area: *craft shops owned by sooth-moothers from Surrey and Knightsbridge*

> This term can be slightly derogatory. It depends who's saying it and to whom!

souch or **sough** (*pronounced* **sooCH**) *verb* usually referring to the wind, to blow or howl noisily: *There's aye a gey cold wind souching down King Street.* | *noun* the noise made by a strong wind: *lying in bed listening to the souch of the north wind in the birks* If you **keep a calm souch** you stay calm or quiet in a difficult situation, without panicking or becoming excited: *Keep a calm souch till the worst is ower, then we'll see what's what.* [Old English **swogan**]

spaewife (*pronounced* **spay**-wife) *noun* a woman who is supposed to be able to foretell the future: *Her pals dared her to go to the spaewife and have her fortune told.* [from the Old Norse]

spaiver or **spaver** (*pronounced* **spay**-ver) *noun* spoken in East the fly on a pair of trousers: *Pull up yer spaiver, it's at half-mast.*

speir (*pronounced* **speer**) *verb* to ask or inquire: *They speirt if I'd seen her.*

spelk *noun* a splinter of wood, especially one which has become embedded in your skin: *He got a spelk in his thumb.*

speug (*pronounced* **spyug**) or **spug** *noun* a sparrow: *A wee speug landed on the table and flew away with a crumb.*

sploonging (*pronounced* **sploon**-jing) *adjective* soaking wet, generally involving puddles of water: *Rain had been getting in through the roof, and the floor was sploonging.*

sprauchle (*pronounced* **sprawCH**-l) or **sprachle** (*pronounced* **spraCH**-l) *verb* to clamber or make your way slowly and with difficulty: *It took her nearly twenty minutes to sprauchle up the brae.*

spurgie (*pronounced* **sper**-gee) *noun* spoken in Northeast a sparrow: *We couldnae sleep for the chirpin' o' a nest o' spurgies.*

stammygaster (*pronounced* stam-mee-**gas**-ter) *spoken in Northeast noun* a shock or unpleasant surprise: *Ah never had such a stammygaster!* | *verb* to give someone a shock or unpleasant surprise: *He was fair stammygastered by the news.*

stank *noun* spoken in Central **1** the gutter at the side of the road: *dead leaves lying in the stanks* **2** a drain at the side of a road, or the grating covering one: *He dropped a pound coin and watched in agony as it disappeared into a stank.* **Down the stank**

means lost beyond all hope of retrieval: *That's mair money doon the stank at that bookies.*

stappit (*pronounced* **stap**-pit) *or* **stappit fu** *adjective* as full as it can possibly be: *Folk say that loch's stappit fu wi fish; Na, nae puddin for me. Ah'm stappit.*

steamie *noun spoken in Central & Southern* an old-fashioned public laundry where people took their clothes and washed them themselves: *My mother used to take her washing to the steamie in an old pram.* Someone or something that is **the talk of the steamie** is very much gossiped about: *If you two keep having lunch together you'll be the talk of the steamie round here.*

steen *noun spoken in North* a stone: *flingin' steens in the watter*

stey (*pronounced* **stie**) *adjective* steep and difficult to get up: *a stey brae*

stoat *or* **stot** *verb* to bounce: *The rain was stoatin off the pavement; She stoated the ball off the ground.*

stoater *noun* something or someone that is an outstanding or exceptional example of its kind: *McLean scored in the last minute with a stoater of a shot from twenty-five yards; See thon blonde lassie works up the stair? A right wee stoater, eh?*

stoatin *or* **stottin** *adjective* so drunk as to have difficulty walking without staggering: *He gets stoatin fou every Friday; Don't you dare come home stoatin again tonight.*

stookie *noun* **1** a plaster cast for a broken limb: *She came back from the hospital with a big stookie on her arm.* **2** someone who is ill-at-ease, out of place or unable to make conversation: *Nobody knew anybody else and we just sat there like a lot of stookies.* [a Scots form of *stucco*, meaning plaster of Paris, or a plaster statue]

stooshie or **stushie** noun a row or uproar, usually in protest: *Plans to redevelop the harbour area have raised a stooshie in the town; Ach, it's no worth making a stooshie about.*

stotter verb To stagger or stumble: *He went stotterin off down the road.*

stour or **stoor** (pronounced **stoor**) noun dust: *The place was full of stour after we cleared the bookshelves.*

stourie or **stoorie** (pronounced **stoo**-ree) adjective dusty: *It's awful stourie under that bed.*

stramash (pronounced stra-**mash**) noun a disorderly commotion or argument: *Two men were arrested following a stramash in a city-centre street in the early hours of Sunday morning.*

stravaig (pronounced stra-**vayg**) verb to wander or roam aimlessly: *It's all right for you, stravaiging about the countryside, but some of us have to work for a living.* | noun a long, aimless ramble or journey: *We just want to go from A to B, not be sent on some daft stravaig all over the place.* [from older Scots *extravage* to wander]

stroupach (pronounced **stroop**-aCH) noun spoken in North a drink of tea: *Ye'll have time to come in for a stroupach?* [from **stroup**, the mouth or spout of a kettle, pump, etc]

sumph noun a stupid, slow-witted person: *It's right in front of ye, ye muckle sumph!*

swack adjective spoken in North fit and supple: *I'm no so swack as I used to be.* [from Flemish]

swatch noun a look at something: *Gie's a swatch at your paper when you're finished wi' it.*

swedger (*pronounced* **swej**-er) *noun* a sweet, such as a mint, toffee or chocolate: *Pass the swedgers round, will you?*

sweetiewife (*pronounced* **swee**-ti-wife) *noun* a person, man or woman, who is very gossipy: *Mind yer ain business, ya pair o' auld sweetiewives!* [originally a woman who sells sweets]

> Apparently the sweetness of these ladies' wares was not reflected in their characters.

sweir (*pronounced* **sweer**) *adjective* unwilling or reluctant: *When it came tae hard work he wasnae sweir.* [from Old Northumbrian *swǣr* meaning lazy]

swick *verb* to cheat or swindle: *Aye, ye were swickit there.* | *noun* a swindle or swindler: *There was naethin in the box ava'. It was naethin' but a swick.*

swither *verb* to be unable to decide or choose: *The board is still swithering about investing many millions in a new ground or renovating the current stadium.* | *noun* a state of indecision: *I'm in a bit of a swither about what to wear.*

syboes (*pronounced* **sie**-beez) *plural noun* spring onions: *Ah says tae the lassie 'See's hauf a pun o' syboes, hen,' an' she looks at us as if Ah wis speakin' double Dutch.* [from French *ciboule*]

synd or **syne** (*pronounced* **sine**) *verb* to rinse something out or give it a quick wash: *Synd oot thae dishes.* | *noun* a rinse or quick wash: *Just gie yer cup a wee synd an' we'll be off.*

syne (*pronounced* **sine**) *adverb* 1 since or ago: *It's mair nor three years syne.* 2 then: *Syne in comes ma mither.*

syver (*pronounced* **sie**-ver) *noun* a drain in a road, or the grating that covers it: *Frankie fun a fiver lyin' in the syver.*

tackety (*pronounced* **ta**-kit-ti) *adjective* referring to footwear, with hobnails or studs in the soles: *a decent pair of tackety boots with steel toecaps*

tait (*pronounced* **tayt**) *noun* a small piece or amount of something: *just a wee tait of sugar in my coffee*

tak tent *phrase* to pay heed to something, to take care: *It's no as easy as it looks, so tak tent.*

tanner ba *noun* literally, a ball costing sixpence (the pre-decimal equivalent of 2.5 pence). In Scottish football, part of the mythology of the 'good old days' is that the best players emerged from poverty, where they learned their skills with no other equipment than the cheapest of balls: *The Lisbon Lions didnae have a' these trainin facilities. A tanner ba was good enough fur them.*

tapsalteerie (*pronounced* tap-sl-**tee**-ree) *adjective, adverb* **1** upside-down: *Sometimes I think the whole world's gone tapsalteerie.* **2** untidy and chaotic, or in an untidy and chaotic way: *Dirty clothes were scattered tapsalteerie around the room.*

tattie (*pronounced* **tat**-ee or **tot**-ee) *noun* a potato: *mince and tatties; It's sair on yer back, howkin tatties.*

tattie-bogle (*pronounced* **tat**-ee-**boe**-gl) *noun* a scarecrow: *He was in old ragged clothes like a tattie-bogle.*

tattie-boodie *noun spoken in Northeast* a scarecrow: *standing out in the field like a tattie-boodie*

tee-name *noun spoken in Northeast* a nickname: *Everybody knew him as Zorba, for that was his tee-name in the Merchant Service.*

telt *verb* the past tense of tell; told: *Ah've no seen it, Ah telt ye.*

teuch (*pronounced* **chooCH** or **chuCH**) *adjective* tough and hard to chew: *This steak's a bit teuch.*

teuchat (*pronounced* **chooCH**-it) *noun* spoken in Eastern a lapwing: *The only sound was the cry of a teuchat high over the field.* [imitating the bird's call]

teuchter (*pronounced* **chooCH**-ter) *noun* a Lowland name for a Highlander, especially a Gaelic-speaking one: *They put up bilingual street signs in Airdrie so that the teuchters down for the Mod could find their way around; a pub frequented by Glasgow's teuchter community*

> Many people think of this term as harmless and chiefly affectionate, but as some Highlanders consider it to be derogatory it should only be used with care among strangers.

thae (*pronounced* **dhey**) *determiner* those: *Post thae letters for me, will ye?*

thirled *adjective* bound to something by obligation, duty or habit: *Scottish public-sector workers are thirled to the British state which pays their wages.*

thrang *adjective* busy, meaning both crowded with people and fully occupied doing something: *streets thrang with shoppers; I'm ower thrang to help.*

thrapple *noun* the throat or windpipe: *Get this doon yer thrapple.*

thraw *verb* spoken in East to twist or sprain a joint or limb: *I've thrawed my ankle.*

thrawn *adjective* awkward and obstinate, often taking delight in being difficult and uncooperative: *That thrawn old devil would* argue black was white; a thrawn inability to agree about anything important

through-other *adjective* untidy, disordered or dishevelled: *The place is just a through-other mess.*

toorie *noun* a round bobble or pompom on a hat: *A woolly hat's not complete without a braw toorie on the top.* A **toorie bunnet** is a hat with a bobble on it, especially a knitted bobble-hat: *Here's a picture of Tom Weir in his toorie bunnet at the top of Goat Fell.* [from **toor**, the Scots form of **tower**]

torn-faced *adjective spoken in Central* having a bad-tempered or grumpy expression: *What's she looking so torn-faced about now?*

totie (*pronounced* **toe**-tee) *or* **tottie** (*pronounced* **tot**-ee) *adjective* very small: *a totie wee baby*

tottie *or* **totty** (*pronounced* **tot**-ee) *spoken in West Central. same as* **tattie**

towsie *adjective* rough and bad-tempered: *It was a towsie relegation battle with no goals but plenty of bookings.*

> The word is especially used to describe a game of football or rugby in which there is little flowing play and many petty (or not-so-petty) fouls.

trauchle (*pronounced* **trawCH**-l) *or* **trachle** (*pronounced* **traCH**-l) *noun* hard work, usually monotonous and unrewarding: *It took years of hard trauchle before he saw any success.* | *verb* **1** to walk or work slowly and wearily: *She trauchled up the brae with her bags of messages; trauchling away at a job he hated* **2** to tire out or exhaust, especially by long hard work: *Make us a cup o' tea. Ah'm sair trauchled after comin up a' thae stairs.*

tumshie (*pronounced* **tum**-shee) *noun spoken in Central & South* a turnip: *She got a casual job lifting tumshies.*

unco (*pronounced* **ung**-ka) *adjective* **1** very or extremely: *The island has a whisky trail for the unco drouthy.* **2** strange or unfamiliar: *an unco sicht* **Unco guid** means excessively religious, self-righteous, or narrow-minded.: *Is Gaeldom populated exclusively by drunks and the unco guid?* [a Scottish variant of **uncouth**]

> One of Burns's best-known poems is the 'Address to the Unco Guid', an attack on the rigidly righteous.

vennel (*pronounced* **ven**-l) *noun* a lane or alley: *We went on a ghost walk through the vennels of Edinburgh's Old Town.* [from French]

voe *noun spoken in Orkney & Shetland* a small bay or narrow creek (often found in place names): *The Isle of Balta all but fills the mouth of the voe; Sullom Voe* [Old Norse]

vratch *noun spoken in Northeast* a despicable or pitiable person: *Ah'm scunnered wi' her behaviour, the dirty vratch!* [a form of **wretch**]

wabbit (*pronounced* **wab**-bit) *adjective* tired, run down, and lacking in energy: *I think I'll have an early night: I'm feeling a bit wabbit.*

wallie *or* **wally** (*pronounced* **wal**-li) *adjective* made of porcelain or glazed china: *She had the regulation pair of wallie dugs on the mantelpiece.*

> In the late nineteenth and early twentieth century, a pair of decorative china dogs or

'wallie dugs' was a standard feature of Scottish living rooms. In twenty-first century, however, most Scots would no longer regard these as a desirable feature.

waur (*pronounced* **war**) *adjective* worse: *I'd be nane the waur o' a long lie in the mornin'.*

wean (*pronounced* **wayn**) *noun spoken in West Central* a child, especially a young one: *Try that if you have four weans and a fat lazy husband; an exchange scheme involving local weans and some pupils from Germany* [a contraction of **wee ane** little one]

Weedgie (*pronounced* **wee**-jee) *noun* a derogatory Edinburgh name for anybody from Glasgow: *Why build a new stadium on the outskirts where it will be easier for Weedgies to get to than the club's own supporters?* [a shortening of **Glaswegian**]

weel *adjective, adverb* well: *He's no awfy weel; He's no weel aff; Take yer wee brither as weel.*

weel-kent (*pronounced* weel-**kent**) *adjective* well known or familiar: *These are weel-kent names to Scotland's real-ale drinkers; Now, there's a weel-kent face!*

wersh *adjective* having an unpleasant taste, whether through being too bland or sour: *Soup made with water rather than stock can be gey wersh; The strawberries were still under-ripe and wersh.*

whaup (*pronounced* **whawp**) *noun* a curlew: *the plaintive cry of a whaup on the muir* [imitation of the bird's cry]

wheech (*pronounced* **wheeCH**) *verb* to move quickly: *He went wheeching down the hill on his bike; The barman tried to wheech my pint away before I'd finished.* [imitation of the sound of something moving rapidly through the air]

wheen *determiner* an indeterminate but reasonably large number or quantity: *There's still a wheen of work to do.*

wheesht or **wheesh** *interjection* be quiet!: *Wheesht till Ah hear this announcement!* | *verb* to tell someone to be quiet: *parents wheeshting their children* | *noun* **Haud your wheesht** means to be quiet: *Would you pair haud your wheesht! Yer argy-bargyin's giein me a headache.*

whigmaleerie (*pronounced* whig-ma-**lee**-ree) *noun* a decoration, trinket, or ornament: *the whigmaleeries and curlie-wurlies of statuettes which adorn the monument*

widdershins (*pronounced* **wid**-er-shinz) or **withershins** (*pronounced* **widh**-er-shinz) *adverb* anti-clockwise or in a direction opposite to the course of the sun: *He made a circling motion widdershins in the air.* [from a Middle High German word meaning opposite course, from **wider** against plus **sin** course]

> Widdershins is traditionally seen as the opposite way from normal, and among the superstitious to do something widdershins is thought to bring bad luck.

wyle *spoken in Northeast verb* to choose: *Ye can wyle yer pick.* | *noun* a choice or selection: *a wyle o' twa hooses* **The wyle** is the best or choice example of something: *She could tak her pick frae the wyle o' them.*

wynd *noun* a narrow street or lane, often a winding one, which leads off a larger or more important street: *the wynds, courts, and closes of the Royal Mile*

yestreen (*pronounced* yes-**treen**) *adverb* last night, or sometimes, more loosely, yesterday: *It was gey wet yestreen.* [a contraction of **yester-**, as in yesterday, plus **even** evening]

yett *noun* a gate: *the prison yett; as daft as a yett on a windy day*

> In place names such as **the Yetts o' Muckhart**, a **yett** is a pass running between hills.

yin *noun* one: *Let's see the ither yin again; Youse yins will have tae wait.*

yirdit *adjective* *spoken in Northeast* dirty: *The bairn was yirdit wi' glaur.* [from **yird**, a Scots word for earth]

yoke *verb* *spoken in Northeast* to start work for the day (or shift): *Are you no yokit yet?*

yowe *noun* a female adult sheep, a ewe: *a park o' breedin yowes wi' lambs*

THE SCOTSMAN

- Explains the meanings and origins of Scottish words and phrases.

- Official and colloquial words with definitions.

- An informative and entertaining guide to modern Scots.

Collins

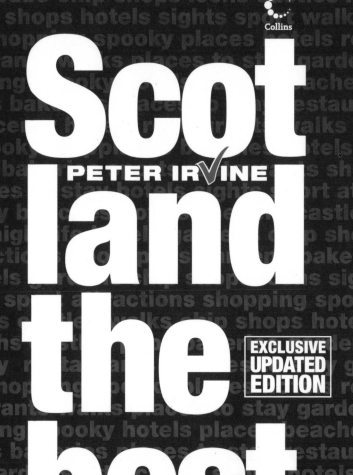

Scot
PETER IRVINE
land
the
best

EXCLUSIVE UPDATED EDITION

Collins

SCOTLAND*on*SUNDAY